HOME SWEET HOME

Igloos

by Betsy Rathburn

BLASTOFF! READERS 1

BLASTOFF! READERS, AN IMPRINT OF BELLWETHER MEDIA BY FLUTTERBEE

Blastoff! Readers are carefully developed by literacy experts to build reading stamina and move students toward fluency by combining standards-based content with developmentally appropriate text.

Level 1 provides the most support through repetition of high-frequency words, light text, predictable sentence patterns, and strong visual support.

Level 2 offers early readers a bit more challenge through varied sentences, increased text load, and text-supportive special features.

Level 3 advances early-fluent readers toward fluency through increased text load, less reliance on photos, advancing concepts, longer sentences, and more complex special features.

★ **Blastoff! Universe**

Reading Level

Blastoff! Beginners — Grade K

Blastoff! Readers — Grades 1–3

Blastoff! Discovery — Grade 4

This edition first published in 2027 by Bellwether Media, Inc.

For information regarding permission, write to Bellwether Media, Inc., Attention: Permissions Department, 3500 American Blvd W, Suite 150, Bloomington, MN 55431.

Library of Congress Cataloging-in-Publication Data

Names: Rathburn, Betsy author
Title: Igloos / Betsy Rathburn.
Description: Minneapolis, Minnesota : Bellwether Media, Inc, 2027. | Series: Home sweet home | Includes bibliographical references and index. | Audience: Ages 5-8 | Audience: Grades 2-3 | Summary: "Developed by literacy experts for students in kindergarten through grade three, this book introduces igloos to young readers through leveled text and related photos"– Provided by publisher.
Identifiers: LCCN 2026011455 (print) | LCCN 2026011456 (ebook) | ISBN 9798898800284 library binding | ISBN 9798898802813 paperback | ISBN 9798898801526 ebook
Subjects: LCSH: Igloos | Inuit–Dwellings | LCGFT: Juvenile literature
Classification: LCC E99.E7 .R22 2027 (print) | LCC E99.E7 (ebook) | DDC 693/.91–dc23/eng/20260225
LC record available at https://lccn.loc.gov/2026011455
LC ebook record available at https://lccn.loc.gov/2026011456

Editor: Rebecca Sabelko   Designer: Andrea Schneider

Printed in the United States of America, North Mankato, MN.

Table of Contents

Keeping Warm

It is cold outside.
This igloo will
keep us warm!

What Is an Igloo?

Igloos are homes made from blocks of snow.

They are usually built in the **Arctic**. This area is very cold in the winter.

the Arctic

Igloos were once used by some **Inuit** people. They were often **temporary** homes.

Size of an Igloo

Inuit people

Inside an Igloo

People enter an igloo through a tunnel. The tunnel can be long or short.

tunnel

The tunnel opens into a **dome**. People live and rest in this room.

dome

The dome has a **vent** near the top. It brings in fresh air.

vent

Some igloos connect to other igloos. More people can gather.

Parts of an Igloo

These **unique** homes are cool places!

Glossary

Arctic

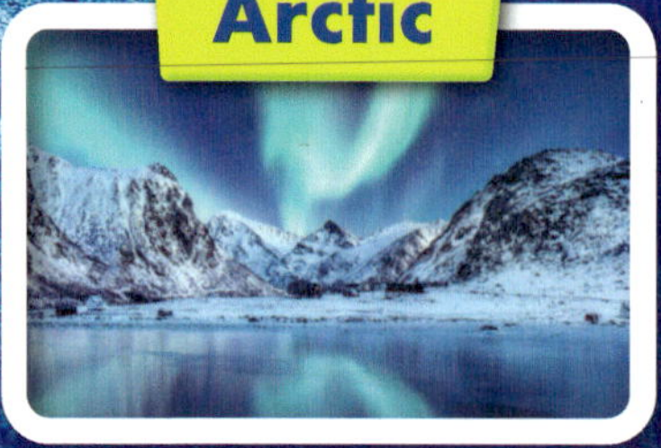

the area around the North Pole

dome

a room with a rounded top

Inuit

people whose relatives have lived in the Arctic since long ago

temporary

only used for a short time

unique

one of a kind

vent

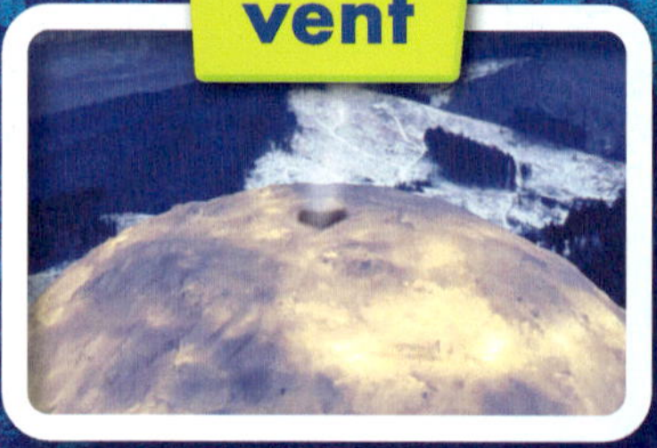

a small hole to help air move

To Learn More

AT THE LIBRARY

Bruegl, Heather. *Inuit*. Ann Arbor, Mich.: Cherry Lake Publishing, 2026.

Phillips-Bartlett, Rebecca. *The Arctic Ocean*. New York, N.Y.: KidHaven Publishing, 2025.

Rathburn, Betsy. *Yurt*. Minneapolis, Minn.: Bellwether Media, 2027.

ON THE WEB

FACTSURFER

Factsurfer.com gives you a safe, fun way to find more information.

1. Go to www.factsurfer.com.
2. Enter "igloos" into the search box and click 🔍.
3. Select your book cover to see a list of related content.

Index

The images in this book are reproduced through the courtesy of: Smitt, front cover, pp. 4-5; Atlas, p. 3 (hat); berkahjayamaterial, p. 3 (snow); ton koene/ Alamy, pp. 6-7, 10-11, 14-15; Jan Garbers, pp. 8-9; zhuxiaophotography, p. 9 (the Arctic); Ivan Kmit, pp. 12-13, 19 (parts), 22 (vent); Aerial Film Studio, p. 13 (inset); Kotenko_A, p. 15 (dome); wanderluster/ Getty Images, pp. 16-17; Andreass96, pp. 18-19; mauro-grigollo, pp. 20-21; biletskiyevgeniy, p. 22 (Arctic); vovashevchuk, p. 22 (dome); Galen Rowell/ Getty Images, p. 22 (Inuit); Nataliia_Makarova, p. 22 (temporary); Evgeniy, p. 22 (unique).